Manfred Aigner

**Best Value Procurement -
The best bid wins the bidding process!**

The advice, tips, and recommendations have been selected by the author with due care and are based on his personal experience. The information provided in this book is for educational and informational purposes only. While the author has made every effort to ensure the accuracy and completeness of the information contained in this book, the author assumes no responsibility for errors, inaccuracies, omissions, or any other inconsistencies herein.

Readers are advised to consult with professionals in the respective fields for specific advice tailored to their individual situations. The author shall not be liable for any loss, damage, or other negative outcomes resulting directly or indirectly from the use of or reliance on the information contained in this book. All actions taken by the reader based on the contents of this book are at the reader's own risk.

The references to external websites or third-party publications were carefully checked at the time of publication of the book. However, subsequent changes cannot be ruled out. The author assumes no liability for the content of these external websites or publications, as this content is not an integral part of this book. The work, including its parts, is protected by copyright. The author is responsible for the content. Any use without the author's consent is prohibited.

ISBN Softcover: 979-8303877078
ASIN E-Book Kindle Edition B0DQJRNTR7

© 2024 Manfred Aigner
All rights reserved. Reproduction only with written permission of the author. Contact exclusively via www.MA-4Consult.at

Content

Introduction 7

1. International failures in public procurement projects 9

    European wind turbines - a market without demand 9
    South Africa - when a bridge has to be built twice 11
    Aerotrain for Kuala Lumpur Intl. Airport - ordered twice 12
    BER Airport in Berlin - Good things take time 14

2. Award procedure according to the best bidder principle 17

    Legal framework and compliance 17
    The supplier's perspective on customer 20
    Unique Selling Point (USP) - a key concept in sales 22
    Procurement process 25
        Phases of the procurement process 26
        Best or lowest bidder 28
    Tender procedure 30
    Tender design and publication 32

3. Best Bidder Procedure: evaluation criteria 37

    Transparency 40
    Requirements for the scope of delivery 40
    Evaluation criterion: Price 42
        Abnormally Low Bid 43
        Formula for price evaluation 46
    Evaluation criterion: Financial capabilities 49
    Evaluation criterion: References and experience 52
    Evaluation criterion: Standards and certifications 56
    Evaluation criterion: Environmental standards and sustainability 57
    Evaluation methodology 60
        Overview 60
        Assessment of evaluation criteria 61

4. Advantages for private and business use 65

5. Epilogue 69

6. Tools and list of sources 71

Introduction

It is likely that many of us have encountered proverbs or phrases such as "**You get what you pay for**" or "**If you buy cheaply, you pay dearly**" These statements are frequently heard, and unfortunately, they are often accurate. Regardless of whether you are considering the purchase of a new vehicle or a government agency is investing in infrastructure, these proverbs can be supported by a variety of case studies.

This book is dedicated to the procurement process, with a focus on the design of corresponding tenders and award processes. The objective is to ensure that the optimal solution or product is purchased at the conclusion of this process. The text employs examples to elucidate the principles of best bidder, as opposed to lowest bidder. The aim of this guide is to provide readers with a comprehensive and practical framework for the implementation of best bidder principles.

For this reason, I would like to proceed with a comprehensive analysis as soon as possible and focus on the content aspects of this book, rather than the usual dedications and paragraphs about the author. Should you require further information about me, I invite you to visit the website www.MA-4Consult.at.

I hope you enjoy reading this book and that you find it informative and helpful.

Manfred Aigner (2024)

1. International failures in public procurement projects

The following section presents a selection of international case studies that illustrate the potential challenges associated with the tendering process in the context of project implementation. These examples demonstrate how deficiencies in the tendering procedures and criteria for supplier selection can lead to delays, cost overruns, and quality issues. The projects presented serve as a reminder of the potential pitfalls and provide insights into the key considerations when awarding public contracts.

European wind turbines - a market without demand

The Austrian Green Party has adopted the slogan "Where there's a will, there's a wind turbine" as part of its strategy to achieve climate happiness in 2023[1]. However, if slogans of this category are not supported by EU-wide strategic measures, they will ultimately prove ineffective and result in empty political rhetoric. Despite the lack of an EU-wide energy strategy and the dominance of regional interests in Germany and Austria, another trend is emerging in these countries. The installation of an increasing number of Chinese wind turbines is creating significant challenges for the domestic and European wind energy sector. While there is considerable potential for wind energy, in a market economy, supply and demand determine price and, therefore, market conditions. Without public tenders to stimulate demand, there is no corresponding supply, which has an adverse impact on the viability of the European wind energy industry.

One might now object that a considerable amount of capital is being invested in wind energy. The veracity of this assertion is contingent upon the specific country or region under consideration. However, it is imperative to question whether the investments being made are being made "properly" or whether the tenders for infrastructure projects are designed in a manner that prioritizes the lowest price as the determining factor, thereby placing European products at a disadvantage in terms of quality. In many instances, European tenders lack "best bidder criteria," which could ensure the procurement of the best quality products through a transparent and competitive award process.

China accounts for approximately **70% of global wind turbine production capacity**, and Chinese companies are increasingly leading the development of efficient offshore wind turbines[2]. Consequently, if public tenders for infrastructure projects in this category are designed in a way that gives significant weight to price, it is not unexpected that European wind energy companies may face challenges.

The proposed system does not necessitate the direct provision of subsidies to companies, nor does it require the implementation of tariffs on non-European products. Both measures have the effect of distorting the markets, increasing government spending due to higher administrative costs, and leading to an increased risk of trade wars. Similarly, European tenders could stipulate a certain local content, i.e., **European added value or production**, in a manner analogous to the "Inflation Reduction Act" passed in the USA in 2022. This approach strengthens European industry through demand from the public sector in accordance with EU law, without the potential waste of taxpayer funds on subsidies, some of which may be unnecessary and unconditional.

The key question in this context is how to apply the best bidder principle in a way that aligns with the principles of a free market economy. This guide will provide guidance on how to achieve this.

South Africa - when a bridge has to be built twice

The Gwaiing Bridge is situated on the N2 road between George and Great Brak in South Africa. Construction of the bridge commenced in January 2018 with an anticipated completion date of July 28, 2020[3]. However, the original contractor, KPMM Roads and Earthworks (Pty) Ltd, encountered financial challenges that prevented them from completing the project by the end of 2023[4]. One of the primary causes of the delays and ultimate failure of the project was the **financial difficulties** experienced by the original contractor, which resulted in **cash flow constraints**. The project's failure resulted in delays, cost increases, and increased administrative costs due to the new tender. Additionally, traffic disruptions for road users and a loss of confidence among citizens in the ability of the responsible institutions to complete projects on time and cost-effectively occurred. Could the risk of the project failing in this way have been avoided? The answer is no. However, the risk of failure could have been minimized.

By designing the tender documents in accordance with the financial capacities of individual providers, it is possible to evaluate the latter apart from the solution or price offered. This additional evaluation criterion is designed to guarantee that providers possess the necessary financial resources to successfully undertake and complete complex and long-term projects. Additional bank guarantees, along with the protection afforded by a corresponding performance bond, serve to provide further security mechanisms.

However, it is preferable to conduct a preliminary selection during the initial award procedure, and it is beneficial if the evaluation criteria of the bids already take financial capacities into account.

Aerotrain for Kuala Lumpur Intl. Airport - ordered twice

The KLIA Aerotrain project, which encompasses the rail link to Kuala Lumpur International Airport (KLIA), represents a significant infrastructure initiative aimed at enhancing connectivity between the main terminal building and the satellite terminal. Initially commissioned in 1998, the Aerotrain system has subsequently confronted a multitude of challenges and delays, ultimately necessitating a comprehensive re-tendering of the project.

The necessity for modernizing of the Aerotrain system was first identified in 2020, when Malaysia Airports Holdings Berhad (MAHB) initiated a tender process for new trains following the completion of several feasibility studies. These studies, conducted in collaboration with various stakeholders, including the Ministry of Transport and the Civil Aviation Authority of Malaysia, recommended a complete renewal of the existing system[5]. In August 2021, MAHB announced that a final shortlist of bidders had been drawn up for this project.

The initial tender was terminated in August 2023 due to delays and performance issues associated with the original contractor, Pestech International Bhd[6]. Pestech encountered a number of specific challenges with the KLIA Aerotrain project, which ultimately resulted in the termination of the contract.

As indicated in publicly accessible documentation, the principal concerns that were identified included[7] [8]:

1. **Performance issues:** Pestech was unable to fulfill the contractual obligations, which resulted in considerable delays in project advancement.
2. **Breaches of Contract:** There were multiple instances of significant non-compliance with contractual obligations, which Pestech was unable to rectify within the specified timeframe.
3. **Failure to Meet Obligations:** Pestech was unable to fulfill its contractual obligations.

These issues led MAHB to question Pestech's capacity to successfully complete the project. The decision to cancel the contract was made with the objective of ensuring the project's completion in an efficient and timely manner. Subsequently, MAHB opted to re-advertise the contract and ultimately appointed a new consortium to oversee the project in January 2024. This example illustrates that the design of the evaluation criteria in the bidding process could have been more meticulous, thus preventing such issues. It is reasonable to posit that the experts responsible for the original award will be required to provide satisfactory explanations for their actions. Such delays to a public project generate, justifiably, a greater degree of media coverage. The issues with Pestech on the KLIA Aerotrain project had political ramifications in Malaysia. There have been public debates and concerns about the award of the project and the government's role in it, despite the fact that the award decision was primarily made by Malaysia Airports Holdings Berhad (MAHB). It can be observed that an effective selection of bidding criteria during the award process can ultimately reduce the risk of potential delivery issues.

BER Airport in Berlin - Good things take time

When a project is completed 10 years late and 300 percent over budget[9], there are a variety of causes that must be identified and addressed. The analysis of the project indicates that the primary source of criticism pertains to the decision to award numerous individual contracts rather than to commission a general contractor who could have assumed the technical and financial risk. This approach resulted in challenges related to coordination and control. When considered alongside inadequate construction supervision and a lack of expertise in certain instances, this resulted in significant delays and additional costs.

As indicated by the Organization for Economic Co-operation and Development (OECD), the BER project did not adhere to the formal bidding process. This resulted in the airport company's systematic contravention of the European Union's (EU) procurement directives. The supplementary work encompassed by these contracts was, in fact, foreseeable to the management team and, thus, ought to have been awarded through a bidding process[10].

The "best bidder principle" could have potentially prevented many of the problems that arose with the BER Airport project. The following are some concrete ways in which the best bidder principle could have helped to mitigate these issues:

- The "best bidder" principle, as opposed to the conventional practice of awarding contracts to the lowest bidder, would have assigned **greater significance to the quality of the bids**. This approach would have ensured that only those providers with a demonstrated history of expertise and experience in complex construction projects would have been considered.

- **Thorough evaluation criteria**: In addition to price, the best bidder principle also considers other significant factors, including technical expertise, sustainability, innovative capacity, and the ability to meet schedules. This approach would have facilitated the selection of providers capable of meeting the rigorous demands of such a project.
- The **best bidder principle** has the potential to minimize planning errors and frequent changes by enabling the selection of the optimal bid based on comprehensive criteria. Providers with robust planning expertise and experience are more likely to be awarded the contract, thereby reducing the likelihood of planning errors.
- **Improved Construction Supervision**: It is probable that vendors selected under the best bidder principle would have implemented superior construction supervision and quality control measures. This would have facilitated the identification and rectification of construction defects at an early stage.
- The best bidder principle encourages a **long-term perspective** that considers the life cycle costs and sustainability of a project. This would have facilitated the selection of providers that are not only cost-effective in the short term but also economical and sustainable in the long term.

The application of the best bidder principle could have facilitated the implementation of the BER Airport project in a more stable and efficient manner from its inception. This approach may have potentially averted the occurrence of delays and complications.

2. Award procedure according to the best bidder principle

Legal framework and compliance

It is of the utmost importance that the legal framework and compliance requirements are adhered to in order to ensure the successful implementation of best bidder procedures. These requirements are designed to guarantee transparency, fairness and equal treatment, as well as to circumvent legal conflicts. The following section provides a comprehensive overview of the key legal requirements and regulations, as well as the measures that have been put in place to ensure compliance.

Ensuring **transparency and equal treatment** is a fundamental legal obligation in the procurement process. Public tenders must be conducted in a manner that guarantees transparency and traceability. This necessitates that all potential bidders are provided with identical information and opportunities. The tendering body is legally required to disseminate comprehensive and accurate information regarding the requirements, selection criteria, and evaluation methods. This guarantees that all bidders possess the same prerequisites and can formulate their bids accordingly.

Another crucial element is the **stipulations of competition law**. In this regard, market access and the prohibition of discrimination are also pertinent considerations.

It is imperative to guarantee that all prospective providers are accorded equal access to the award procedure, without any distinctions being made on the basis of nationality, company size, or other characteristics. Moreover, antitrust regulations must be adhered to. Agreements or arrangements that impede competition, such as price fixing or market sharing, are prohibited and can result in significant legal ramifications.

The consideration of **environmental and social standards** represents another crucial element. Contracting authorities are legally obliged to take environmental and social standards into account in their procurement procedures. This can include, for example, the consideration of ecological criteria or minimum social standards. Contracts may only be awarded to companies that comply with these standards in order to ensure sustainable and socially responsible procurement.

Documentation and reporting obligations represent further essential components of the legal framework. It is necessary to meticulously document all stages of the procurement procedure in order to be able to present the decision-making processes in a comprehensible manner in the event of complaints or audits. In some jurisdictions, there is an obligation to report the award procedures and their results to higher-level bodies in order to ensure transparency and accountability.

In order to guarantee adherence to the legal framework and to circumvent potential legal disputes, it is essential to implement a series of measures. The importance of **internal training and awareness-raising** cannot be overstated in this context. By providing regular training for all personnel involved in procurement procedures, organizations can foster a comprehensive understanding of the legal requirements and the significance of compliance. Furthermore, awareness campaigns within the organization can assist in highlighting the potential risks and consequences associated with non-compliance.

The utilization of **compliance tools and systems** can also facilitate the assurance of compliance. Compliance management systems (CMS) are employed to monitor and regulate compliance with legal requirements and internal guidelines. Electronic procurement platforms enhance transparency and facilitate compliance with procurement rules.

The implementation of regular **external and internal audits** represents a further measure to ensure compliance. These audits serve to monitor compliance with the legal framework and identify potential deficiencies at an early stage. In order to ensure their effectiveness, it is essential that the procedures undergo regular review and adaptation in accordance with new legal requirements and best practices.

Moreover, the establishment of transparent and well-defined **procurement guidelines and processes** is of paramount importance. The development and implementation of comprehensive internal guidelines and procedures for the implementation of procurement procedures play a pivotal role in ensuring consistency and compliance. The use of standardized templates for tenders and evaluation forms serves to guarantee compliance.

Effective **contract management** and monitoring are also crucial elements. The implementation of robust contract management strategies ensures that contractors adhere to their contractual obligations. The establishment of prompt mechanisms for addressing infringements or complaints during the award process helps to prevent legal disputes.

By taking into account the specified legal framework conditions and implementing effective compliance measures, contracting authorities can ensure that the procedures for determining the most economically advantageous tender are transparent, fair, and legally compliant. This not only serves to avoid legal conflicts but also promotes public and supplier confidence in the procurement process.

The supplier's perspective on customer

In the context of a sales representative's role in a company, it is reasonable to assume that the objective is to establish contact with potential clients and to negotiate agreements that will result in sales. In order to engage in discourse regarding prospective business cases with prospective customers, it is imperative to ascertain the customer's needs and to identify the areas where the customer is experiencing difficulties. The capacity to cultivate and sustain a relationship of trust with the customer is of paramount importance for success. This proximity to the customer, referred to as "customer intimacy," when coupled with effective relationship management, represents a critical success factor.

In order to ascertain a customer's requirements, it is advisable to adopt a methodical approach. In B2G business, the "follow the money" principle can serve as a useful guide.

In practical terms, this means that you should monitor budgets and investment projects in the public sector. If you or your company have established a positive customer relationship, you will be aware of these issues in your discussions with customer representatives. This does not necessarily require an appointment with the board; you can often be heard at the working level.

Alternatively, you can also work effectively with the standard product and solution life cycles in your business environment and industry. Typically, you are aware of the last time your customer procured a specific product or solution from you or one of your competitors. Given your knowledge of the duration of such installations, you can estimate the timeframe for the next procurement or replacement of these applications.

In the event that a particular requirement on the part of the customer has been identified, it is advised that the "solution mode" is not immediately engaged. In the technical field, there is a tendency to respond rapidly to problems with proposed solutions. The issue is that there is no guarantee that the ad hoc solution will yield the optimal benefit for the customer. In such cases, it is advisable to adopt a consultative approach, employing communication techniques from the domain of consultative selling to ascertain the scenario that will offer the greatest benefit to the customer. Only by focusing on the customer's best interests can a competitive advantage be secured.

In the context of tenders in which the best-bidder principle is applied, additional evaluation criteria are employed by the tendering bodies that extend beyond the mere bid price. It should be noted that there are numerous additional award procedures. The Austrian Federal Procurement Act enumerates a total of eleven distinct award procedures[11]. Globally, the pertinent public procurement legislation serves as the foundation for successful B2G sales. It is prudent to consult with legal experts versed in the current legal landscape of the target country to gain insight into the prevailing legal framework. In such instances, local representatives from the home country or local partners can be consulted for guidance. It is important to note that in certain circumstances, there is a choice between "restricted" award procedures and direct awards. These variants can be particularly advantageous for suppliers in the context of existing customer business. These "simplified" awards are also advantageous for the awarding authority, as every public invitation to tender entails a considerable amount of work and therefore costs for the tenderer. When discussing the topic of "budget" with customers or interested parties, it is also important to address the "internal costs" of tendering procedures. This will ensure that potential customers do not overlook their budget planning and that appropriate consideration is given.

Unique Selling Point (USP) - a key concept in sales

In the process of developing an optimal solution for prospective customers, the objective is to guarantee the greatest benefit for the customer and to identify distinctive selling points. The term "unique selling point" (USP) is often misunderstood. A USP is, by definition, "unique," and the customer is willing to pay (more) for it. The concept of uniqueness can only be evaluated in relation to that of the competition; otherwise, there is no basis for comparison or for the application of the term "unique." Furthermore, the term "selling" can only ever refer to specific customers who also invest budget in certain topics and functionalities. Consequently, there can be no USP that has no reference to competitors and customers. Therefore, the term USP should not be used in a general and generic way and certainly not be mentioned as a USP in general marketing brochures. In most cases, these are features or functions that are not automatically a USP.

In the event that a colleague inquires as to the unique selling proposition (USP) of product A, it is recommended that the following questions be posed: With which customer and in comparison to which competitor? In essence, the individual terms can be arranged in a logical sequence as follows: Pain ↔ Feature ↔ Benefit.

Unique Selling Point (USP) - a key concept in sales

The customer pain point or need is addressed with a bespoke solution or product comprising a number of features and functions. The provision of individual features and functions may confer a distinctive benefit to a specific customer. These aspects are of critical importance with regard to the functionality of the targeted solution, as their relevance for the customer largely determines their classification. In the absence of this benefit, the corresponding functions are regarded as mere "nice-to-have" features. If they are features and functions that cannot be offered by the competitor in its portfolio, they are considered unique. In this case, these are "unique features" with direct customer benefits, but not yet a unique selling proposition (USP). Only if the customer is willing to pay a premium for this benefit and thus for this functionality compared to the competitor's solution, which cannot offer this functionality, can we speak of a USP.

In the event that a product is in direct competition with other providers and the product in question possesses only a few unique features or lacks certain functionalities that are of great importance to the customer, it would be prudent to consider whether it would be feasible to expand the solution through active cross-selling. This entails incorporating additional elements from the company's product portfolio into the proposed solution. Rather than offering a single product that directly competes with existing alternatives, it may be possible to identify other areas of customer need that can be combined with each other. This approach could allow for the inclusion of one or two products in the solution that are not currently available from competitors.

To illustrate this concept, we will utilize a fictitious example from the automotive industry. In the event that Tesla wishes to sell your company several vehicles for your company fleet, it can be considered as a potential supplier of electric vehicles in conjunction with other suppliers. Should Tesla demonstrate their in-house Superchargers[12] to your fleet management team and they determine that they are advantageous, Tesla can offer you more than simply vehicles. Given that you may have been planning to purchase charging stations on your premises anyway, but did not consider procuring them from the same supplier as your new vehicles, Tesla has provided you with an additional benefit. Consequently, Tesla has a distinctive selling point that other providers who only offer electric cars do not possess. In this scenario, Tesla can circumvent a competitive situation with potentially more cost-effective suppliers of electric cars.

The above example demonstrates the importance of maintaining a continuous, consultative dialogue with potential customers. The initial solution strategy for the aforementioned issue would be for automotive manufacturers to present their model range and make corresponding offers based on this presentation. It is possible that you were not aware that you had another need, namely charging stations. For Tesla, this could be a way to avoid a price battle with other car suppliers. The company could offer new cars for the company fleet and charging stations for the company premises from a single source. However, this would require Tesla to be aware of the demand.

The aforementioned example leads to the following explanation, which focuses on the formulation of needs and requirements.

Procurement process

The primary objectives of a procurement process can be summarized as follows:

- ✓ The objective is to procure the **right product**.
- ✓ The product must **meet the required specifications**.
- ✓ The **evaluation** must be conducted in an **appropriate** manner.
- ✓ The objective is to identify the supplier that can **best meet** the organization's **needs**.

If all four areas are answered with a clear "yes" or "done," it is reasonable to expect that the optimal solution for an existing requirement will be identified by the end of the day.

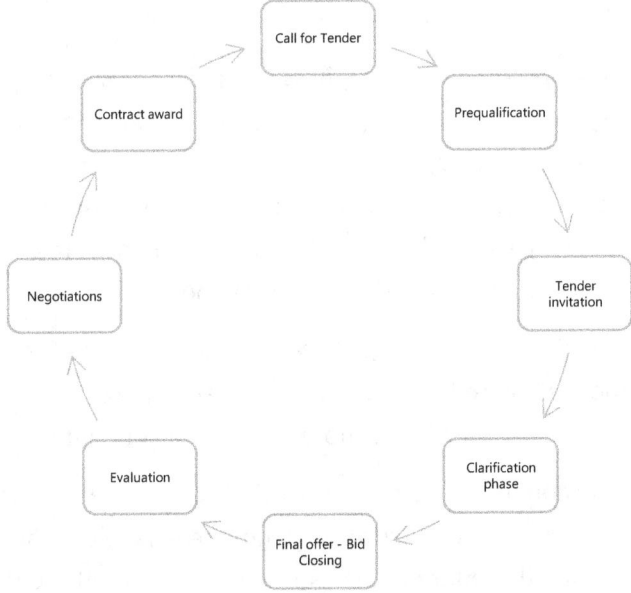

The procurement process is comprised of a series of phases and stages. At the outset, the focus is on defining the requirements, selecting the award procedure to be utilized, and defining the evaluation criteria according to which the contract is awarded. This procedure ensures the necessary transparency.

Phases of the procurement process

The **invitation to tender** represents the initial formal step in the procurement process, which serves to obtain offers from potential suppliers or service providers. In this phase, the procuring entity defines the requirements, specifications, and conditions of the project in detail. An adequately conducted tender creates transparency and competition, which can ultimately lead to an optimization of bids. It is essential to provide all relevant information to enable bidders to have a clear understanding of the requirements. In practice, tenders are published in publicly accessible media to ensure the widest possible reach and participation.

In the **pre-qualification** phase, an initial assessment of potential providers is conducted to ascertain their fundamental suitability and performance. The objective of this phase is to reduce the number of applicants to a group that meets the minimum requirements. Criteria such as financial stability, technical competence, references, and experience can be utilized in this assessment.

The objective of pre-qualification is to guarantee that only those providers who are both serious and qualified are invited to submit bids, thereby reducing the subsequent evaluation effort.

Subsequent to the pre-qualification phase, the qualified bidders are formally invited to **submit comprehensive bids**. This invitation contains all the information required to prepare the bids, such as specifications, schedules, contract terms, and evaluation criteria. The providers are then afforded the opportunity to present their solutions, prices, and conditions in detail. As clear and precise communication is crucial at this stage to avoid misunderstandings and ensure that the submitted bids meet the requirements, a careful and structured approach is required.

The **clarification phase** commences immediately upon the submission of tenders and serves to elucidate any open questions and eliminate ambiguities. During this phase, both the procuring entity and the bidders are afforded the opportunity to request or provide additional information. The objective of this phase is to guarantee that all offers are complete and comprehensible. This may entail formal presentations and negotiations to gain a deeper understanding of the details of the bids and make any necessary adjustments.

Once the clarification phase is complete, bidders are typically requested to submit their **final bids**, which encompass all modifications and clarifications that have been discussed. This final bid submission represents a pivotal stage, as it determines the definitive terms and prices that will be included in the evaluation. At this juncture, bidders are afforded the opportunity to optimize their bids and enhance their competitiveness.

As part of the **evaluation phase**, the final offers are subjected to a systematic review and assessment based on the previously defined criteria. These criteria may include, for example, price, quality, delivery time, technical competence, and other relevant factors. The evaluation is typically conducted by a team of experts who assess the bids independently and objectively. The objective is to select the bid that offers the greatest overall value, taking into account both economic and qualitative aspects.

Following the evaluation, there is an opportunity to **negotiate** with the preferred provider to clarify the final details of the contract and potentially secure more favorable terms. This stage is crucial to ensure that both parties fully understand and accept all aspects of the contract. Potential areas for discussion include discounts, delivery terms, or additional services. A successful conclusion to the negotiations results in a clear and binding contract.

The **awarding of the contract** signifies the formal conclusion of the procurement process. The selected provider is then officially notified, after which the contract is signed. At this juncture, all pertinent internal and external stakeholders are duly informed. The awarding of the contract frequently entails an announcement of the decision, a measure designed to ensure transparency and to apprise the other providers of the outcome. Once the contract has been awarded, implementation of the project or delivery of the goods or services commences in accordance with the agreed conditions.

Best or lowest bidder

The fundamental issue in all procurement processes is whether a public tender, which is typical for B2G/B2B business cases, is based on the "best bidder" principle or the "lowest bidder" principle. This question can also be applied to private use, for example, when purchasing a new vehicle, a house, or a modern laptop.

The term "**Best Value Principles (BVP)**" appears to be a more precise designation, as it places greater emphasis on the value of a product or solution.

The lowest bidder principle is based on the evaluation of bidders primarily on the basis of the bid price. In this case, the lowest bidder is awarded the contract. An extreme example of this variant can be found in many public tenders in India, where bidders are obliged to fulfill all the requirements of the tender (so-called "100%

compliant"). Subsequently, they must compete against their competitors in a so-called "reverse auction." In consequence, it can be asserted that the bidder offering the lowest price will invariably emerge triumphant in this process. This is attributable to the fact that bidders are compelled to undercut one another in order to secure the contract. One disadvantage inherent to this format for the tendering body is that, in the event that the requirements are not sufficiently delineated, providers who are unable to meet the requirements, for example in a complex B2G project business, may also participate.

It is possible that you have already had experience with the construction of a house or other craft services in a private environment. However, if an imprecise specification is made and the price is used as the sole evaluation criterion, problems can quickly arise that were not intended in advance and lead to additional costs. This is because the theory that buying products or services at a low price ultimately leads to higher costs has been confirmed many times in practice, both in a private context and in the context of procurement projects in the business sector.

In accordance with the best bidder principle, the bid price is weighted in such a way that it is not included 100% in the evaluation. Typically, the share of the price in the evaluation falls between 30% and 70%. Consequently, the price is an award criterion that is supplemented by other criteria.

Tender procedure

When acquiring products or services, there are typically multiple avenues for structuring the tendering process.

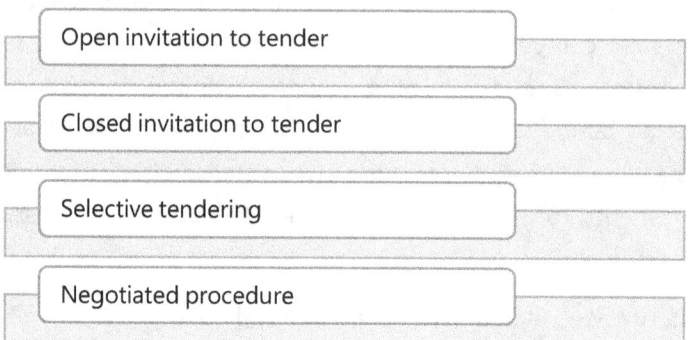

Open tendering is a procedure in which a public announcement is made inviting all interested suppliers to submit a bid. This procedure is often used for public contracts (B2G business) to ensure transparency and competition. All potential providers are invited to apply, which results in a broad selection of offers.

Advantages	Disadvantages
Transparency: Public announcement ensures all interested providers receive the same information and have the same opportunities.	An open tender can be a **time-consuming** process, as it often requires the review of numerous bids.
Competition: The open invitation to tender encourages competition, which can result in more favorable pricing and terms.	**Cost:** The administrative and review processes associated with the numerous bids can be financially burdensome.
A **diverse range of options** allows clients to identify the optimal solution.	**Quality:** There is a risk that bids may be submitted by providers with limited experience or inadequate qualifications.

As part of a **closed invitation to tender**, the invitation to submit a tender is issued exclusively to selected bidders. This procedure is used in particular when the contracting authority already has a list of qualified bidders and wishes to ensure continuity in the composition of the bidders.

Advantages	Disadvantages
Quality: By limiting the number of providers invited to submit bids, we can ensure that only high-quality submissions are received.	Due to the exclusive nature of the invitation process, **competition may be constrained**, potentially resulting in elevated pricing.
Efficiency: The review of tenders is less time-consuming as only a limited number of tenders are submitted.	**Restricted selection:** The number of bids available for consideration is limited, which constrains the ability to identify the optimal solution.
Confidentiality: The closed call for tenders allows for more confidential negotiations as fewer providers are involved.	There is a **potential for bias** on the part of the client, who may favor certain suppliers.

Selective tendering is a hybrid of open and closed tendering. The process begins with a public announcement to which interested providers can respond. This is followed by a pre-selection of the most suitable providers, who are then invited to submit a bid.

Advantages	Disadvantages
Quality and competition: This process encourages the highest standards of quality and competition, as only the most qualified bidders are invited to submit a bid.	The pre-selection process is **time-consuming** and should be factored into the overall project timeline.
Efficiency: The pre-selection of suppliers streamlines the process by reducing the number of bids to be reviewed, enhancing overall efficiency.	**Costs:** The administration of the pre-selection process and the subsequent tender review may result in additional costs.
The client has the **flexibility** to adjust the pre-selection criteria to ensure that only qualified suppliers are included in the process.	**Transparency:** There is a risk that the pre-selection process may not be as transparent as an open tender.

The **negotiated procedure** is a special form of contract award in which the client negotiates directly with one or more providers in order to achieve the best possible conditions. This procedure is often used for complex or specialized projects that require close cooperation between the client and provider.

Advantages	Disadvantages
The negotiated procedure allows clients to negotiate the terms of the contract directly with suppliers, providing greater **flexibility**.	Due to the fact that only a select group of providers are involved in the negotiations, **competition** may be somewhat **limited**.
Adaptability: The client is able to consider specific requirements and changes during the course of the negotiations.	The negotiated procedure is **less transparent** than an open tender, as negotiations take place behind closed doors.
Quality: By negotiating directly, the client can ensure that the providers possess the requisite qualifications and experience.	**Time-consuming:** The time required for negotiations can be considerable, particularly for complex projects.

Tender design and publication

When establishing an award procedure, it is crucial to clearly define the award criteria and the associated procedure. The following quote from Benjamin Franklin provides a useful guideline: "**The bitterness of poor quality remains long after the sweetness of low price is forgotten.**"

It is important to consider the economic aspect, including the bid price from different providers, when evaluating tenders. However, focusing exclusively on price while neglecting the quality and capabilities of the providers may lead to dissatisfaction in the long term.

The specific tendering procedure may vary, but in all typical B2G cases, it can be assumed that suppliers will submit bids. In this context, the question arises as to how one becomes aware of published tenders. In the event that a potential provider engages in an effective opportunity development phase, it can be assumed that the provider also possesses the requisite knowledge regarding the timing and modalities of the tendering of an award project by a potential customer. This allows for the avoidance of unexpected developments and ensures that the provider is adequately prepared.

In this context, it is important to consider how interested parties can access information about published or planned tendering procedures if they have not yet had any direct contact with the tendering institutions. As previously stated, B2G business typically involves publicly advertised tendering procedures. This ultimately facilitates awareness of tenders and participation in them. In this context, the Internet is also an excellent source of information. In many cases of B2G business, tenders are published by public authorities, public sector companies, or companies in the public sector environment, either directly on their own homepage or on the homepage of the relevant ministry. In some countries, there are also tender portals operated by the administration that publish all public sector tenders.

It would be remiss not to mention the tender portals in Europe, of which those provided by the EU or the European Bank for Reconstruction and Development (EBRD) are prime examples. The EU portal[13] allows users to create search profiles that enable targeted searches for tenders for specific goods and services, filtered by country and customer. The EBRD portal[14] operates on a comparable premise, with an emphasis on EBRD-backed procurement initiatives. A notable benefit of both portals, that of the EU and that of the EBRD, is that in numerous instances, the ultimate contract award is also disclosed. This allows for the identification of pricing from competitors who have secured a contract.

Private providers also claim to list all tenders worldwide. There are undoubtedly reputable providers on this market, but a certain degree of sensitivity is required when providing data as part of a registration on the aforementioned portals. It is recommended to use portals of administrations, governments, or, as previously mentioned, the EU. For an overview of local tender portals in various countries worldwide, please refer to the World Bank's homepage (Global Public Procurement Database [15]), which also provides country-specific data.

It is important to acknowledge that the process of screening tender databases, even with the application of filters, requires a certain degree of effort. Unless the potential supplier or a representative from the sales department performs these tasks themselves, it is recommended that a designated individual within the company be assigned the responsibility of screening tenders. This role does not necessitate a full-time commitment, but it is advantageous for the individual to possess knowledge about tenders and to dedicate the requisite time to this task. The decision regarding participation in the tender process can be made at a later date. However, it is crucial to ascertain in advance whether there are any relevant tenders for the company in question. In the event of a positive decision, it is essential to possess detailed knowledge of the specific contents of the tenders.

If you are planning a tender as a potential customer and not as a bidder, you are subject to **public procurement law** in the B2G sector. Public procurement law sets out the procedures and conditions that contracting authorities must take into account when carrying out their procurement measures. The objective of public procurement law is to guarantee transparency, competition, and equal treatment throughout the procurement process, while also promoting the efficient use of public funds. It is essential that procurement procedures are transparent and fully documented. The fundamental principles include the publication of invitations to tender, the disclosure of selection criteria and the documentation of decision-making processes. It is vital to ensure that all bidders are treated equally and are protected from discrimination. This implies the **evaluation of tenders according to previously defined criteria** in a fair and objective manner. It is the responsibility of the awarding authorities to ensure fair competition. This is accomplished by establishing suitable tender deadlines and eliminating unnecessary impediments for potential bidders. The requirements and conditions of the tender must be commensurate with the subject matter of the contract. It is essential to exercise caution to prevent disproportionate requirements that could result in the unnecessary exclusion of bidders. As part of the award procedure, requirements regarding sustainability and innovation can be imposed. One way to achieve this is by incorporating environmental standards and social criteria into the tender evaluation process. It is the responsibility of the awarding authorities to ensure that all relevant national and, in the case of tenders in the EU, European regulations are complied with. This includes both procedural rules and specific legal standards, such as labor law and environmental protection regulations. Furthermore, mechanisms must be provided that enable bidders to file a complaint in accordance with the law if they believe that the award procedure was flawed or that their rights have been violated.

These elements serve to guarantee a fair and efficient public procurement system that serves the common good and prevents the misappropriation of public funds.

Despite the generally slow pace of change in the B2G sector and the tendency for new developments to be gradual, it seems reasonable to assume that this area will continue to evolve. Those who establish the direction of future developments can anticipate subsequent adaptation processes, which are typically time-sensitive. Such processes are often fraught with difficulties and require significant effort and resources. The challenging circumstances brought about by the global pandemic have led to unprecedented adaptations in many sectors, particularly in the public sector and B2G. One notable example is the adoption of digital signatures for contract closure with public sector entities, a practice that was previously unheard of.

The design of tenders and the definition of the criteria for evaluating bids are pivotal elements in the procurement of services. It is not feasible to present a universally applicable version here, as the criteria and their design are highly contingent on the underlying business. Depending on the requirements of the tendered solution, some criteria may be deemed irrelevant or a different weighting should be applied. The following table provides examples of possible criteria for tenders in the solution-based project business, including a potential weighting.

Evaluation Criteria	Potential weighting
Bid Price	30 – 70 %
Financial capabilities of the bidder	10 – 15 %
Experience of the bidder	5 – 10 %
Necessary certifications	5 – 10 %
Technical and functional requirements	10 – 30 %
Other criteria	5 – 10 %

3. Best Bidder Procedure: evaluation criteria

The best bidder procedure, also referred to as "best value procurement," has its roots in the nineteenth century and was initially implemented in the United Kingdom. The objective of this procedure is to broaden the scope of evaluation beyond mere price to encompass qualitative and economic considerations. This approach was necessitated by the need to establish a fair and transparent method for the awarding of public contracts. Over the course of the 20th century, the best bidder procedure was adopted in numerous countries around the globe. The proliferation of this procedure was enabled by the increasing globalization and the implementation of modern procurement methods. Consequently, the best bidder procedure was adapted in a multitude of countries, including the United States, Germany, France, and numerous other European and non-European countries. Currently, the best bidder process is utilized in a considerable number of countries globally, particularly within the European Union, where it is regulated by various directives and regulations. The objective is to advance sustainable and innovative solutions that are economically, socially, and environmentally beneficial.

It is encouraging to note that the use of a **best bidder procedure** is permitted in **numerous industrialized nations across the globe** and is also backed by corresponding legislation. Consequently, the best bidder procedure can be employed in countries such as the United States, Canada, the Netherlands, Norway, Poland, Austria, the Czech Republic, Botswana, Saudi Arabia, Malaysia, India, and Australia.

The evaluation of tenders represents a critical juncture in the contract award process. The criteria employed serve as a pivotal determinant in the identification of the most optimal provider. It is essential to strike a balance between the consideration of cost aspects and the selection of the most suitable provider.

Other frequently mentioned criteria in tenders include delivery time, delivery period, layout/design or usability, customer service, service after the warranty has expired, an additional warranty, and environmental characteristics. Additionally, criteria such as energy consumption and the quality of the offer, including documentation, can be considered. There are no limits to creativity in this regard.

The following examples illustrate other criteria that could be used in the course of a procurement process:

- As part of the tender submission process, the bidder is required to describe how the proposed solution aligns with and supports the sustainability goals of the user and their organization.
- The quality, completeness, and descriptive level of detail of the offer will be assessed based on various criteria. Firstly, the completeness of the topics covered will be considered. In addition, the clarity of the explanations, the legibility, and the support provided by appropriate evidence will be assessed.
- The bidder is required to provide suitably qualified personnel to carry out the required work. Additionally, the bidder must submit the curricula vitae of the personnel who will be carrying out the contract.

A significant challenge in procurement projects is the discrepancy between the customer's expectation of receiving the optimal value and the design of the tender or the award criteria. To guarantee that the optimal bidder criteria are genuinely implemented and that customers receive the desired "best value," they must be an integral component of the tender requirements and evaluation criteria. Over the past decades, the best bidder procedure has become a highly effective method for achieving optimal overall values for public contracts. The consideration of quality, performance, and sustainability aspects in conjunction with costs encourages the development of innovative and long-term advantageous solutions.

Transparency

It is evident that a multitude of criteria can and, in many instances, should be employed. It is my contention that the most crucial element of tenders conducted in accordance with the best bidder principle is the **assurance of transparency and openness**. Nevertheless, the efficacy of the criteria is constrained if they are not effectively disseminated. The fundamental requirement for a transparent tendering process is the disclosure of the evaluation criteria, which must be included in the tender documentation. This is typically accomplished in the introductory section of a public tender. Moreover, the results of the evaluation must be communicated to the providers once completed. This process should be the primary objective for any type of tender to ensure fair competition. A transparent approach is particularly crucial for tenders in the public sector, as in this domain, tendering bodies frequently operate with public funds, which are often financed by tax revenues.

I would like to take this opportunity to express my personal opinion on the matter. It is my belief that taxpayers have a right to be informed about the criteria used to procure public funds. The findings of the Parliamentary Committee of Inquiry into the German freeway toll project[16] demonstrate the importance of transparency in the awarding of public contracts and the use of public funds.

Requirements for the scope of delivery

The focus of consideration in every procurement process is the product, solution, or service to be procured. It should be noted that there are specific problem areas and needs that are considered particularly relevant by customers and that need to be addressed; otherwise, there would be no rationale for initiating a procurement process.

Accordingly, the specifications are included in a comprehensive tender package, which is a mandatory requirement for all prospective bidders. Bidders' offers are based on the specified requirements. It is reasonable to assume that bidders will normally offer what is required, but no more. In contrast, there are instances where customers have specific, time-sensitive requirements, as well as optional features that may not be essential but could enhance the customer experience.

The **"MUST/SHALL"** and **"SHOULD"** designations within the specification document provide a clear delineation between these two categories.

It is recommended that the mandatory items be clearly stated as "MUST" requirements. All providers must comply with these requirements, as there are certain topics and areas that are essential for the customer. It is preferable to limit the number of "MUST" requirements to a minimum, as this reduces the number of potential providers. An example of such a requirement would be the procurement of a car, where the car must have four wheels. Suppliers who cannot fulfill this requirement are immediately excluded from further evaluation and, thus, from the procurement process. This should be noted in the tender documents.

The aforementioned functionalities, the implementation of which is not mandatory but would yield additional benefits for the customer, can be formulated as "CAN/SHOULD" requirements in the requirements document. In this case, the respective bidder will not be excluded from the further procurement process if the stated requirements are not met. The bids will be evaluated in accordance with the other evaluation criteria. However, it is recommended that these "CAN/SHOULD" requirements be supported by corresponding evaluation points. This implies that bidders who present solutions that fulfill the aforementioned requirements will also receive corresponding evaluation points. The "CAN/SHOULD" criteria should be assigned a **weight of approximately 10 to 30 percent** within the overall evaluation. When compared with the requirements for the service to be offered, this value appears relatively low. However, this can be explained by the fact that the evaluation criteria are only the "nice-to-have" requirements, as the urgently needed requirements are already anchored in the tender as "MUST/SHALL" requirements.

Evaluation criterion: Price

The evaluation of price is an essential criterion for the selection of the most advantageous offer, and a comprehensive process that requires the consideration of various influencing factors. The focus is usually on CAPEX costs (i.e., procurement costs). However, more recently, there has been a shift towards the evaluation of OPEX costs (i.e., ongoing operating costs). This requires suppliers to disclose and include follow-up costs, such as maintenance costs, in their offers.

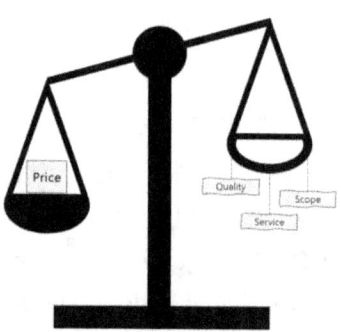

In applying the best bidder criteria, it is of the utmost importance to ensure a balanced relationship between price and quality. One common method is to weight the evaluation criteria with a share of approximately 30% for price. By limiting the price weighting to around 30%, it is ensured that the bids are evaluated holistically, taking into account both the price and other key criteria such as quality, service, and performance in an appropriate manner, and preventing them from becoming "lightweight."

Abnormally Low Bid

In certain countries, the practice of utilizing providers that offer unfairly low prices through the tendering process is prohibited due to the fact that the formula utilized for price evaluation is either non-linear or that a minimum price is established which must not be undercut. The lower limit is based on market studies conducted in advance by the tendering body. In the event that this limit is not reached, the respective bidder is not awarded any points for the price criterion, or is excluded from the subsequent award process. This approach effectively precludes the inclusion of dumping providers in a meaningful evaluation.

> It is recommended that the evaluation of prices exclude those offered by providers who are known to engage in dumping practices.

In response to concerns about the potential for abnormally low bids (ALB) in public procurement procedures, some countries within the EU have already implemented measures to prevent the lowest bidders from being selected.

The **World Bank** defines abnormally low bids as follows: While an abnormally low bid may initially appear to represent a favorable value, it may ultimately result in a higher price for the total cost, contract delays, or even failure of the contract. Contractors who frequently submit ALBs may be unable to complete their work at the agreed price, or may have made errors in their bids that prevented them from completing the work at that price[17].

European public procurement law (Directive 2014/24/EU of the European Parliament, for example Article 69) also stipulates that tenders that fall into this category may be disqualified from the subsequent award process. In the event that the tenderer is unable

Best Bidder Procedure: evaluation criteria

to provide sufficient justification for its bid price, the contracting authority is entitled to reject the tender. Furthermore, rejection should be mandatory if the contracting authority finds that the proposed prices or costs are abnormally low and result from non-compliance with mandatory Union social, labor, or environmental law, or national legislation that is in conformity with Union law or international labor law provisions[18].

The question thus arises as to how one might identify abnormally low bids. There are a number of different approaches to this, with the majority of cases falling into one of two categories: the "absolute" approach or the "relative" method.

In accordance with the so-called "absolute" method, the tendering body is responsible for preparing its own cost or price estimate. This is based on the question of what costs can typically be estimated on the market for the tendered solution. The individual tender prices are then set in relation to their own market price estimate. In the event that the bid price falls below a previously defined threshold, for example 50% below the bidder's own market price estimate, and there is no plausible explanation from the bidder, these bids can be classified as "abnormally low bids."

The "relative" method is founded upon statistical calculations, whereby all bids received are taken into account. Consequently, this method is only applicable when a minimum of three to five bids have been submitted. A potential "abnormally low bid" is identified when a price is more than the statistical standard deviation below the average price of all submitted bid prices. However, when employing this method with the application of mathematical and statistical procedures, it is essential to ensure that all prices were set competitively, independently, and in line with market prices.

In accordance with the Federal Procurement Act in **Austria**, the suitability of the prices submitted must be evaluated if they are not aligned with comparable empirical values or relevant market conditions[19].

A comparable provision can be found in the **German** procurement regulations [20]. In the event of a notable disparity between the price or costs proposed and the service to be provided, the contracting authority is entitled to request a corresponding examination or clarification from the bidder. This is a mandatory obligation for the contracting authority, which is not at liberty to exercise discretion as to whether it carries out a clarification. The assessment of whether a tender is abnormally low can be conducted, for instance, by comparing it with the other tenders received[21].

In **Portugal**, the "relative" method is used to determine whether a tender price is abnormally low. This is defined as a price that is below 40-50% of the budget price set by the contracting authority, also known as the base price[22]. The contracting authority may set different irregularity thresholds, but is required to provide this information to potential bidders in advance, as outlined in the tender documents.

The **Polish** Act on Public Procurement permits a comparable approach in Poland. In the event that the offered price, costs, or their essential components appear unusually low in relation to the subject matter of the contract, impair the subject matter of the contract, or give rise to doubts on the part of the contracting authority as to the fulfillment of the contract, the contracting authority is entitled to request the contractor to provide explanations, including the submission of evidence for the calculation of the price or costs. This also applies to documents specified in the invitation to tender or resulting from separate provisions. In Poland, a limit of 30% is applied as part of the "relative" methodology described above[23].

A comparable process was employed in **Italy** until 2023, though five distinct reference/threshold values were permitted (legal basis: Decreto Legislativo 18 aprile 2016, n. 50, Artikel 97). The selection of the calculation method was determined by lot, ensuring that the parameters and thresholds for potential disqualification were not predetermined for the bidders. The new tender law in Italy no longer allows for this innovative approach[24]. However, it does cite EU Directive 2014/24, which provides the option of excluding providers engaged in unfair pricing practices from the subsequent award process, as outlined in Article 110 ("Offerte anormalmente basse").

> Ask local lawyers, procurement portals, or interest groups about ways to prevent abnormally low bids and dumping price bidders in your country.

Formula for price evaluation

Given the continued significance of price in many tenders, even when "abnormally low bids" are already excluded, I would like to offer a suggestion regarding price evaluation:

> It is inadvisable to make price evaluations in a linear fashion, or at the very least, to consider lower price limits!

In a linear price formula for price evaluation, the cheapest provider is awarded 100% of the weighted points, while the most expensive provider does not automatically receive 0%. Rather, the percentage value by which it offered a higher price is assigned as the value for which the most expensive provider is awarded. If the most expensive provider has offered 100% or more more expensive, this provider is awarded zero points.

An alternative approach is to employ a formula in which the evaluation points are not calculated linearly, but in a different function. This results in a rating for providers that are in close competition with each other that is similar in terms of price. Consequently, other qualitative evaluation criteria become more important.

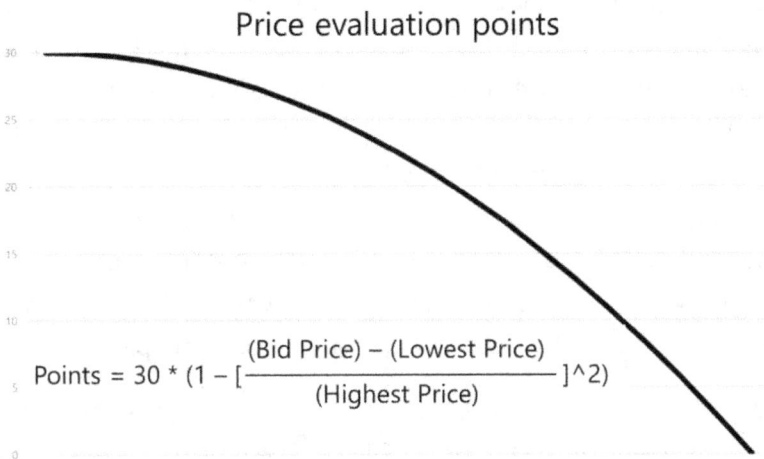

$$\text{Points} = 30 * \left(1 - \left[\frac{(\text{Bid Price}) - (\text{Lowest Price})}{(\text{Highest Price})}\right]^2\right)$$

The example above demonstrates the points curve resulting from an assumed weighting of the offer price at 30%. This indicates that the maximum number of points that can be achieved is limited to 30. However, the most expensive provider is not automatically awarded zero points, even if it were more than 100% more expensive.

The formula presented in this example employs three key variables: the price to be evaluated ("bid price"), the price of the least expensive supplier ("lowest price"), and the price of the most expensive supplier ("highest price"). These variables are then used to establish a relative ranking between the evaluated price and the prices of the two suppliers.

Best Bidder Procedure: evaluation criteria

The rationale behind my recommendation of this particular formula is as follows: The response to this inquiry is relatively straightforward. The tendering body can thus preclude bidders who are characterized by the practice of dumping prices from attaining an unattainable number of points during the price evaluation. Even with a price weighting of only 30%, a linear formula can result in the best bidder having a point gap of 30 points after the price evaluation compared to low-cost bidders, which cannot even be close to being made up with the other evaluation criteria. As a result, the best bidder procedure would effectively become the lowest bidder procedure once more. Other bidders would have no opportunity of winning the contract, even if the remaining criteria were evaluated in their favour. This would effectively render the qualitative criteria null and void. Consequently, the tendering body would be compelled to select a provider who offers the lowest price as its supplier.

The following table illustrates the application of the aforementioned formula to four fictitious providers, with a presumed weighting of 30% for price within the total set of evaluation criteria.

Bidder / Price	Percentage points (max. 30)
Bidder 1: 25 USD	22,5 Percentage points
Bidder 2: 10 USD	30,0 Percentage points
Bidder 3: 30 USD	16,7 Percentage points
Bidder 4: 13 USD	29,7 Percentage points

A comparison of the bidders reveals that the bidder with the lowest price receives the highest score. Conversely, it can be observed that the bidder with the highest price (in this example, #3 with USD 30) still achieves a score of 16.7 points.

To illustrate, consider the following example: In the context of public procurement, the entity responsible for issuing the invitation to tender is bound by the stipulations set forth in the award criteria. In the event that this is not done, it is highly probable that objections and even legal proceedings will ensue. Such an outcome is not in the interests of any of the parties involved, including the tendering companies and the suppliers involved. In order to guarantee compliance with the procurement rules and evaluation criteria, it is necessary to consider the potential for "unfair" market participants or providers to exploit these within certain framework conditions. To illustrate, a public authority may commission the construction of a new administrative building and subsequently issue a tender. However, it is important to ensure that no single provider, regardless of their reputation, is awarded the contract based on the price criteria to the extent that they gain an unfair advantage. This approach can prevent price dumping by unscrupulous providers. To guarantee consistent and intelligible application, the formula should be incorporated into the tender documentation.

In order to ensure a robust and fair process for determining the most advantageous bid, it is essential to develop a comprehensive set of evaluation criteria for the price evaluation area. This should entail a combination of measures designed to prevent abnormally low bids and a non-linear price evaluation formula. This will provide a solid foundation for the best bidder determination process.

Evaluation criterion: Financial capabilities

In order to provide the tendering body with the assurance that **suppliers are sufficiently stable and experienced** to meet the specified requirements, it is essential to inquire and evaluate company-related information. It is important to acknowledge that there have been instances in the past where contracted companies have exceeded their capabilities, both in the B2G segment and in the private sector. For instance, kitchens or houses were ordered and paid for, but the supplier ultimately became insolvent.

A small company may encounter liquidity and cash flow issues due to an order that exceeds its annual turnover. For procurements of high criticality to the customer or with a high potential order volume, a **weighting of 10 to 15%** is recommended within the overall criteria catalog of the offer evaluation.

It is recommended that a validation model or system, also known as a "**financial scorecard**," be used. This is based on an assessment using predefined financial parameters and threshold values. The evaluation can be calculated on the basis of factors such as turnover, profitability, capitalization, liquidity, and debt ratios. These models serve to standardize the evaluation process and provide an objective comparison of bidders. They also form the basis for the final, weighted evaluations of the bidders within this category.

> In the financial evaluation of bids submitted by larger companies, groups, or consortia, it is essential to ensure that the same criteria are applied to all bidding companies, including the respective bidding legal entity, and not just to one (main) bidder or group of companies.

The stated requirements or criteria may pertain to a minimum equity ratio, minimum net assets, liquidity ratios, annual turnover, or the demonstrated capacity to procure performance or financial guarantees (e.g., bank guarantees).

The following criteria serve as an illustrative example of the aforementioned requirements:

- In order to guarantee financial stability throughout the implementation and delivery of the program, the bidding company is required to demonstrate an equity ratio of over 25% in each of the previous five years.
- The annual turnover of the last three financial years should be at least five times the bid price, thus preventing the bidder from becoming dependent on a single order.
- In order to guarantee the seamless processing of orders, bidders and manufacturers are required to exhibit a positive EBIT margin of over x% across the entirety of the previous five years, in addition to a profitable forecast for the forthcoming two financial years

Upon fulfillment of the requisite conditions, the bidders receive the corresponding evaluation points as part of the bid evaluation process. As part of the evaluation process, it is essential to ensure that the criteria are based on verifiable facts. This can be achieved by requesting relevant evidence from the bidders as part of their tender documentation. Alternatively, the tendering body can independently obtain information about the bidders to ensure the accuracy of the information provided.

Bidders may be required to submit **audited financial statements**, including balance sheets, profit and loss accounts, and cash flow statements. The objective is to evaluate the financial health, liquidity, profitability, and solvency of the bidder. Furthermore, questionnaires may be utilized to ascertain the financial capabilities of the bidders. These questionnaires may inquire about the bidders' turnover, capital structure, borrowing capacity, credit lines, and any outstanding debt. It is recommended that self-declarations and questionnaires be employed only in exceptional cases. Instead, audited and certified annual financial statements and statements from auditors should be the primary sources of information.

Procurement agencies have the option of obtaining **creditworthiness information** on bidders from independent rating agencies. This information provides an independent assessment of the bidder's creditworthiness and financial stability. The credit rating assigned to the bidder serves as an indicator of its financial standing. In contrast to the aforementioned variant, where bidders are required to enclose certain documents with their bids, this variant involves a certain amount of work for the tendering body. However, the advantage of this variant lies in the independence of the data and facts.

The objective of these financial evaluation criteria is to guarantee the financial stability and autonomy of the bidders' individual proposals. This guarantees that customers can be reassured that the risk of supplier default due to financial difficulties is mitigated.

Evaluation criterion: References and experience

It would be optimal for the bidder to have prior experience with orders or projects of a similar nature. It is in the client's interest to evaluate the bidder's past performance on similar contracts. The aim of this evaluation is to reduce the risk of non-performance by ensuring that the contractors have comparable experience. It can be assumed that experience minimizes the risk, which is why a **weighting of approximately 10%** is recommended for this evaluation category.

Specifically, this phase of the evaluation focuses on the following core areas:

- ✓ Bidders are required to demonstrate that they have previously successfully implemented contracts of a similar nature.
- ✓ It is incumbent upon the bidder to demonstrate the implementation of previous orders and their operational status.
- ✓ Letters of reference from customers must be provided.
- ✓ It must be possible to visit existing reference customers on site.

As part of the evaluation process, bidders are required to submit a comprehensive **list of similar contracts** that they have completed in the past. This must include detailed information on the respective projects, such as the project name, scope, duration, contract value, and customer information. The evaluation of the information provided by the bidders enables the assessment of their relevant experience in the implementation of projects of a similar type or size. Subsequently, the procuring authority is authorized to evaluate the relevance of the bidder's previous projects to the current procurement, taking into account various factors, including project complexity, industry focus, geographic location, and size.

It is imperative that only those projects and programs that have been successfully implemented and are accompanied by a corresponding acceptance certificate from the customer are accepted as references. Furthermore, no programs may be accepted as references if they are designated as "work in progress" or "in progress," indicating that they have not yet been fully completed.

The tendering body establishes a set of criteria by which the bidder's past performance is assessed. It is essential to assign specific ratings or points to each criterion in order to ensure a standardized evaluation process. As part of the verification process, it is essential to ensure that the information provided by the bidder is accurate and valid. It is essential to verify that the information provided by the bidder regarding its experience and references aligns with the facts. The evaluation process includes a review of the project details, client information, and results to ensure the accuracy and reliability of the results. The various criteria shall be weighted in terms of relative importance in the specific procurement process to ensure a comprehensive evaluation that considers all relevant factors. The final scoring for each bidder will be based on their experience and reference assessment, taking into account the weightings assigned to the performance criteria. However, the focus should be on **comparable contracts with comparable clients** in the recent past (e.g., over the last five years).

Contact with the reference customers provided by the bidders, typically former customers or partners, is essential to ensure a valid assessment of the written reference information. Such contact allows for the assessment of the experience that the reference customers have had in working with the bidder or potential supplier. As part of the preparation for the reference visits, it is recommended that a series of specific questions be drafted which address the bidder's performance, adherence to deadlines, quality of services, communication, and general satisfaction. The type of procurement will determine whether it is appropriate to conduct site visits to the client's customers. If this is the case, the visits can provide first-hand validation of references and verification of the quality of work, compliance with standards and performance against contract content. It is recommended to prioritize contacting references that match the scope, industry or complexity of the current procurement. This will provide more relevant insights for assessing the bidder's capabilities. The following are some examples of how to design requirements for this evaluation category:

- **References:** The bidder must demonstrate experience in delivering at least three programs with similar functionality, complexity, and size within the last five years. These programs must have been successfully implemented and accepted by the customer for operation. Preference will be given to countries neighboring the tendering office. The bidder must submit letters of reference issued by the customer. Additionally, the bidder must be able to facilitate on-site reference visits to existing customers.
- **Contract fulfillment:** Bidders must demonstrate a proven track record of successfully completed contracts. The bidder is required to provide comprehensive details on any legal disputes, arbitration proceedings, or contract terminations resulting from contracts that the bidder has concluded in the past five years or is currently executing.
- **Sanctions:** To mitigate the risk of potential suppliers being investigated by government authorities, bidders are prohibited from conducting business and operating in countries subject to international sanctions by the USA and the EU. This restriction particularly applies to the country of the bidder's incorporation. The list of countries and companies subject to sanctions can be accessed on official US and EU portals.

One particularly challenging evaluation criterion in this category is the assessment of any **past legal disputes and/or contract terminations**. An example of an appropriate evaluation criterion for bidders is as follows: If a contract has been terminated within the past five years, this must be included with the bid in detailed form. Bidders are required to submit declarations on previous contract terminations, which must contain information on the respective client and the reason for termination.

Evaluation criterion: Standards and certifications

In order to guarantee compliance with specific standards, providers may be required to **submit the corresponding certificate**. The evaluation category is designed to ensure an optimal price-performance ratio and first-class quality. This is done in accordance with the applicable legal obligations and standards. It is recommended that **approximately 10%** of the evaluation category be allocated to this.

It is crucial that all certifications required for a tender be applicable to all bidders, including potential subcontractors and/or consortium partners. Otherwise, there is a risk that essential components of the delivery may not meet the required standards. As part of the tender process, it is possible to require bidders and their partners to submit and attach certain certificates. These include, for example:

- ✓ ISO-9001 (quality management)
- ✓ ISO-27001 (information security)
- ✓ UK Cyber Essentials (cyber security)
- ✓ ISO-14001 (environmental management)

As part of the tender submission process, bidders are required to provide certificates issued by an **independent certification body**. Additionally, bidders may supplement the list of certificates with further regional or industry-specific certificates, provided that they are relevant to the ongoing procurement process.

Evaluation criterion: Environmental standards and sustainability

The subject of the "**green economy**" is undoubtedly a megatrend at the present time. Products and solutions that support or exemplify this trend are therefore essential. If you or your company were to develop aircraft with diesel engines and propellers, for example, you would be acting contrary to the technological trends (e.g., biokerosene) on the one hand and the reduced need for (business) travel, especially after the coronavirus pandemic, on the other. Consequently, you would be faced with a market where demand for your product is either low or non-existent. These trends are part of the broader "green economy" megatrend. In Europe, this will result in a further decline in demand for short-haul flights. Consequently, the target market for the propeller aircraft mentioned above will continue to contract. These flight connections will be replaced by high-speed rail or solar-powered aircraft, which will undoubtedly make the "green economy" a megatrend affecting numerous products and solutions across most industrial sectors.

It is recommended that companies which consider the topic of a "green economy" and CO_2 savings to be important first ascertain whether measures have already been taken in this direction. If this is not the case, it would be prudent to refrain from marketing the products and solutions as green. In the end, these companies will be required to provide explanations and evidence for the green "coating" of their products and solutions. If such an explanation cannot be provided, or is only provided inadequately, there is a risk that the company will be associated with **"greenwashing."** It is challenging to maintain a defensive stance in this argument. In the future, the extent to which companies can demonstrate their alignment with sustainability criteria will be a key factor in the awarding of public contracts. In the European Union, this process was initiated several years ago and is known as **"Green Public Procurement."** [25]

This term refers to a process whereby public authorities seek to procure goods, services, and works that have a lower environmental impact throughout their life cycle than goods, services, and works with the same main function that would otherwise be procured. It is imperative for companies, particularly those in the B2G sector, to anticipate that in the near future, public tenders will not permit the practice of "greenwashing." I therefore recommend that companies implement a realistic yet ambitious green strategy if they have not already done so. Suppliers have an essential role to play in helping organizations achieve their sustainability goals. They can do this by integrating sustainability aspects into their order processing, applying sustainable practices, and providing environmentally friendly products and services.

While many procurement authorities are committed to sustainability, they have observed a tendency among bidders to engage in "greenwashing" strategies. In light of these considerations, it is important to determine which focus areas tendering authorities should prioritize in order to facilitate a fair and objective evaluation of bidders. The definition of evaluation criteria serves to mitigate the risk of "greenwashing."

- ✓ **Sustainable solution design:** Solutions offered should be developed with sustainability in mind. This is achieved by integrating energy-efficient technologies, renewable energy sources, materials with a lower environmental impact, and waste reduction strategies into the solution design.
- ✓ **Life cycle thinking** is a crucial aspect of solution design and implementation. It is essential to consider the environmental impacts throughout the entire life cycle of the product, including the stages of raw material extraction, production, transportation, use, and disposal at the end of the product's life. The solution should be optimized in a way that minimizes negative environmental impacts in each phase.
- ✓ In the context of **energy efficiency** and resource optimization, it is essential to optimize energy efficiency in the solution design. This can be achieved by integrating energy-efficient devices, systems, and controls.
- ✓ Effective **waste management** must be implemented as part of the order processing procedure, including the implementation of adequate recycling practices.
- ✓ It is vital for businesses to **record and document key environmental indicators**, such as energy consumption, emissions, waste generation, and resource use. This information is essential for effective environmental management. Communicating sustainability successes and results to customers and stakeholders is crucial for internal and external communication.
- ✓ It is essential to ensure compliance with all applicable **environmental regulations**, laws, and standards.

✓ It is essential that clear environmental policies are communicated within the organization. Environmental management systems, such as **ISO 14001 certification**, ensure effective environmental performance management and continuous improvement.

Evaluation methodology

Overview

A variety of methods exist for the evaluation and assessment of offers. The choice of approach depends on the objective and context of the evaluation, with both quantitative and qualitative techniques employed.

Quantitative methods prioritize the analysis of numerical data and figures. Cost-benefit analysis is an illustrative example of this approach. It entails the quantification of both the costs and the potential benefits associated with an offer, thereby facilitating an informed decision-making process. A comparable method is value analysis, which involves the evaluation of all relevant costs and potential savings, taking into account the total life cycle costs.

In contrast, **qualitative methods** are based on subjective assessments and expert opinions. One example of this is the Delphi method, in which experts provide their opinions anonymously in order to reach a joint assessment. Another method is utility analysis, in which qualitative criteria are converted into numerical values to create an objective basis for comparison.

A common practice in business is to **benchmark** offers against best practices or leading competitors. This allows for a more accurate assessment of an offer's quality and effectiveness. Potential risks and uncertainties are identified and quantified as part of the risk assessment. A common method is **risk analysis**, in which these factors are taken into account in order to minimize their influence on decision-making. Sensitivity analysis can also be used to examine how changes in assumptions can affect the final result.

Multi-criteria methods are particularly useful when evaluating multiple criteria. The analytical hierarchy process breaks down complex decisions into a hierarchy of criteria and evaluates them in pairs. The multi-attribute utility theory calculates the utility values of different alternatives to enable a comprehensive evaluation. The price-performance ratio is also an important aspect. Here, the **ratio of price to service** provided is compared to identify the most economical offer.

The methods presented provide a robust framework for evaluating offers in diverse contexts. The selection of methods should align with the specific application, considering their respective strengths and weaknesses. In the context of the **best bidder procedure** for public tenders, a **combination of some of the presented methods** is utilized. The subsequent chapter elucidates the effective application of the evaluation criteria presented in this chapter.

Assessment of evaluation criteria

It is essential to define and weight the evaluation criteria in a careful and objective manner to ensure a fair and balanced decision in the award procedure. This guarantees that the decision aligns with the project's requirements and objectives in the most optimal way. The weighting should reflect the relevance and importance of each criterion for the specific project or plan. Criteria that are crucial to the project's success should be weighted more heavily. Incorporating feedback and opinions from relevant stakeholders can help to better determine the weighting. This could be done through workshops, surveys, or Delphi methods, for example.

Best Bidder Procedure: evaluation criteria

Evaluation criterion	Weighting	Methodology
"Must" scope of supply	N/A	100% fulfillment /disqualification
Scope of supply "Should"	30 %	Scorecard (points)
Price	30 %	1. exclusion of ALB offers
Financial capability	10 %	2. non-linear evaluation formula
References and experience	10 %	Scorecard (points)
Standards and certificates	10 %	Scorecard (points)
Environmental standards	10 %	Scorecard (points)

"Must/shall" requirements are non-negotiable, essential conditions of a tender. Failure to fulfill these requirements will result in immediate exclusion. "Can/should" requirements are desirable characteristics that will be taken into account when selecting the best offer. However, these requirements do not necessarily have to be fulfilled. This distinction can be applied to all evaluation criteria. The next step is to determine how the fulfillment of different "should" requirements and the bidders' responses will be evaluated. One solution is to create a scorecard with differentiated scoring. The points achieved should then be multiplied by the weighting applied in each case.

Evaluation of the bidder's response	Points
Exceeds the requirement with added value. The offer answers the requirement precisely and relevantly.	10
Meets the requirement. Comprehensive reference in terms of details and relevance to the requirement is included.	8
Meets the requirement in most aspects. Acceptable level of detail and accuracy is provided.	5
Does not fulfill the requirement or only to a limited extent. There is limited further information or limited response to queries.	2
The requirement is not met and questions remain unanswered.	0

Similar methodologies can be found in numerous online sources[26]. This allows a bespoke evaluation matrix to be created. The difference between the best and next best score (e.g. "Excellent" vs. "Good") shows what bidders need to include in the bid to get the best score. In this example, the bidder must exceed the requirements and add value. This evaluation method provides an additional dimension to the evaluation of the bid with the best price-performance ratio (in addition to the weighting of the criteria).

The **disclosure of evaluation criteria and methodology** ensures that the tendering process is fair and equitable. Transparent communication of these aspects strengthens trust in the process. Bidders are aware of the expectations and can be confident that their bids will be evaluated objectively and consistently. This mitigates the risk of accusations of bias or discrimination and fosters fair competition.

Furthermore, **transparency** allows bidders to develop targeted and efficient bids. When the evaluation criteria and methodologies are known in advance, bidders can showcase their strengths and capabilities in the most effective way and tailor their bids to align with specific requirements. This increases the quality of the bids submitted and simplifies the selection of the best bid.

It is also crucial to ensure **compliance with legal and regulatory requirements**. In many countries and industries, tenders are subject to legal regulation, which requires transparent and fair implementation. Disclosing the evaluation criteria and methodologies helps to meet these legal requirements and reduces the risk of legal consequences.

> ℹ Transparency is a critical factor in the success of any tendering process!

Transparency is an effective means of ensuring the **efficient use of resources**. By communicating requirements and evaluation procedures in a clear and accessible manner, bidders can better assess their ability to meet the requirements before investing time and resources in preparing a tender. This reduces the number of unsuitable or inadequate bids and saves both bidders and tenderers valuable time and resources.

A transparent and open presentation of evaluation criteria and methodologies in tenders offers significant advantages for all parties involved. It fosters fairness and trust, enables the preparation of high-quality tenders, ensures compliance with legal requirements, and contributes to the efficient use of resources. An open and transparent tendering process follows the principle that all bidders are informed of the evaluation results for each category. After a standstill period, there is an opportunity for any objections. And after this process, the procurement authority awards the contract to the best bidder. This makes it easier to achieve the main objectives of a procurement process:

- ✓ The objective is to procure the **right product**.
- ✓ The product must **meet the required specifications**.
- ✓ The **evaluation** must be conducted in an **appropriate** manner.
- ✓ The objective is to identify the supplier that can **best meet** the organization's **needs**.

4. Advantages for private and business use

The history of public tenders and projects is replete with instances where mismanagement and a lack of transparency have precipitated political scandals. These scandals not only erode citizens' trust in the government but also result in significant financial losses for taxpayers. There are numerous instances where public tenders or projects have given rise to political scandals.

The construction of **Berlin Brandenburg Airport (BER)** is a case study in how mismanagement and a lack of transparency can turn a public project into a political scandal. Another example of a public construction project that resulted in significant financial and political challenges is the **Elbphilharmonie concert hall in Hamburg**. Another example of a public infrastructure project that resulted in significant cost overruns and political controversy is the **Stuttgart 21 rail project**. Implementing a best bidder process could have helped to select the most qualified bidders. These would not only have had to offer the lowest price, but also the highest quality and reliability. This would have avoided a cost explosion and delays.

The above examples demonstrate that inadequate transparency and insufficient evaluation criteria in public tenders and projects increase the risk of significant political and financial scandals. The application of the best bidder procedure, which considers qualitative criteria as well as price, could have helped to prevent these scandals in many cases and strengthen citizens' trust in public administration.

Advantages for private and business use

It is therefore essential that public tenders are conducted transparently and fairly to select the best bidders and protect the interests of taxpayers.

In both our private and professional lives, we are faced with a multitude of decisions on a daily basis, where we must select the optimal option from a range of alternatives. The best bidder principle, which ensures transparency and quality in public tenders, can also be a valuable tool in the private sector.

Let us consider the following scenario: you are planning a comprehensive **renovation of your own home**. Rather than selecting the lowest-priced option, it is advisable to consider the best bidder principle. In addition to price, quality of materials, experience of craftsmen, and reliability are also factors in the decision. If the sole criterion for selecting a tradesperson is price, the result is often unsatisfactory. This is due to inferior workmanship and additional costs for reworking. By contrast, the best bidder principle ensures that the work is of high quality and has long-term durability.

The decision to purchase **insurance**, whether for health, automobiles, or residences, is a significant one that requires thorough consideration. Selecting the least expensive car insurance may result in complications if the insurer provides inadequate service and delays processing in the event of an accident. To guarantee optimal coverage in the event of a claim, it is prudent to apply the best bidder principle and consider not only the costs but also the coverage, customer service, and reputation of the insurance company.

Childcare is a significant responsibility for parents, who naturally want to ensure that their children are in good hands. Selecting a less expensive childcare option can prove disadvantageous if the quality of care is found to be inadequate. In such instances, the lowest bidder principle may not be the optimal approach. To identify a childcare facility that offers not only competitive pricing but also high-quality and secure services, it is recommended to apply the best bidder principle and consider various factors, including the qualifications of the caregivers, the pedagogical approach, and the equipment.

Applying the best bidder principle in the private sector allows you to make decisions that are not only cost-effective in the short term, but also advantageous and of high quality in the long term. In addition to price, quality, reliability, and any additional benefits, all other factors should be taken into account when deciding on a bid. This will ensure that you receive the best products and services for your needs. The best bidder principle helps you to minimize financial risks, achieve satisfactory results in the long term, and increase confidence in your decisions.

5. Epilogue

I am pleased to hear that reading this book has provided you with new ideas and approaches. This was the fundamental objective when writing it. The book was not intended to be a scientific work, but rather to offer you practical, hands-on assistance.

Naturally, the majority of the topics covered in this publication can be explored in greater detail. I would therefore like to extend an invitation to engage in a dialogue with you. To this end, please visit the website (www.MA-4Consult.at) or follow the social media channels listed there to receive the latest updates free of charge. Should you wish to discuss a specific topic in more depth, you will also find a corresponding contact form on the homepage.

If you have already forgotten much of the content of this book, please recall the core message: act with transparency and openness, both as a buyer and as a customer.

Epilogue

6. Tools and list of sources

The following tools were utilized during the period between November 27th, 2024 and December 16th, 2024:

- Microsoft Copilot: https://copilot.microsoft.com
  (assists with the development of the text structure)
- DeepL Write: https://www.deepl.com/de/write
  (some text passages have been partially reworded)

All of the following sources were thoroughly reviewed at the time of the book's publication. However, it should be noted that changes may have been made at a later date. Internet sources were retrieved between November 27, 2024, and December 13, 2024.

1	Kurier (09th March 2023). "Wo ein Wille, da ein Windrad": Grüne wollen Klimaglück entfachen. URL: https://kurier.at/politik/inland/wo-ein-wille-da-ein-windrad-gruene-wollen-klimaglueck-entfachen/402357756
2	Neue Zürcher Zeitung (30th October 2024). Erst Solarzellen und Elektroautos, jetzt Windräder? Wieder will China dem Westen den Rang ablaufen. URL: https://www.nzz.ch/wirtschaft/erst-solarzellen-jetzt-windraeder-china-draengt-auf-den-weltmarkt-ld.1854753
3	George Herald (20th December 2021). Gwaiing bridge contract to resume next year. URL: https://www.georgeherald.com/News/Article/Local-News/gwaiing-bridge-contract-to-resume-next-year-202112200947
4	George Herald (16th November 2023). Gwaiing bridge re-tender process starts in 2024. URL: https://www.georgeherald.com/News/Article/Local-News/gwaiing-bridge-re-tender-process-starts-in-2024-202311150328
5	Soyacincau (20th June 2024). New KLIA Aerotrain to be ready by 31 Jan 2025. Why did it take so long? URL: https://soyacincau.com/2024/06/20/klia-aerotrain-now-scheduled-jan-2025-why-taking-so-long/
6	New Strait Times (21st August 2023). MAHB shuts door on reinstating Pestech as KLIA aerotrain contractor . URL: https://www.nst.com.my/business/2023/08/945420/mahb-shuts-door-reinstating-pestech-klia-aerotrain-contractor%C2%A0
7	The Star (16th August 2023). MAHB terminates Pestech's RM742.95mil aerotrain contract. URL: https://www.thestar.com.my/business/business-news/2023/08/16/mahb-terminates-pestechs-rm74295mil-aerotrain-contract
8	The Malaysian Reserve (16th August 2023). MAHB terminates RM743m KLIA Aerotrain contract with Pestech over non-performance. URL: https://themalaysianreserve.com/2023/08/16/mahb-terminates-klia-aerotrain-project-contract-with-pestech-due-to-non-performance-and-delays/
9	Euronews (31st October 2020). Berlin airport opens 10 years late and three times over budget. URL: https://www.euronews.com/2020/10/31/berlin-airport-opens-10-years-late-and-three-times-over-budget
10	OECD (2015), Effective Delivery of Large Infrastructure Projects: The Case of the New International Airport of Mexico City, OECD Public Governance Reviews, OECD Publishing, Paris. URL: https://www.oecd.org/content/dam/oecd/en/publications/reports/2015/11/effective-delivery-of-large-infrastructure-projects_g1g6035f/9789264248335-en.pdf
11	WKO. Arten der Vergabeverfahren. URL: https://www.wko.at/service/wirtschaftsrecht-gewerberecht/Arten-der-Vergabeverfahren.html
12	Tesla. Supercharger. URL: https://www.tesla.com/de_at/supercharger
13	Europäische Union (o.D.). Ted – tenders electronic daily. URL: https://ted.europa.eu/TED/main/HomePage.do

14	European Bank. e-Procurement Portall ECEPP. URL: https://ecepp.ebrd.com/delta/noticeSearchResults.html
15	World Bank. Global Public Procurement Database. URL: https://www.globalpublicprocurementdata.org/gppd/
16	Handelsblatt (28th May 2020). „Ein Alexander Dobrindt scheitert nicht" – So kam es zum Chaos um die Ausländer-Maut. URL: https://www.handelsblatt.com/politik/deutschland/untersuchungsausschuss-ein-alexander-dobrindt-scheitert-nicht-so-kam-es-zum-chaos-um-die-auslaender-maut/25869026.html
17	The World Bank (July 2016). Abnormally Low Bids and Proposals – Guide to the identification and treatment of Abnormally Low Bids and Proposals. URL: https://thedocs.worldbank.org/en/doc/780841478724671583-0290022017/original/ProcurementGuidanceidentificationandtreatmentofAbnormallyLowBidsandProposals.pdf
18	Europäische Union. Directive 2014/24/EU of the European Parliament and of the Council of 26 February 2014 on public procurement and repealing Directive 2004/18/EC Text with EEA relevance. URL: https://eur-lex.europa.eu/legal-content/EN/TXT/?uri=celex%3A32014L0024
19	Bundesvergabegesetz 2018. Paragraph 137. URL: https://ris.bka.gv.at/GeltendeFassung.wxe?Abfrage=Bundesnormen&Gesetzesnummer=20010295
20	Vergabeverordnung – VgV. Paragraph 60. URL: https://www.gesetze-im-internet.de/vgv_2016/__60.html
21	Deutsches Vergabeportal. Ungewöhnlich niedrige Angebote. DTVP Deutsches Vergabeportal GmbH URL: https://dtvp.de/info-center/vergabelexikon/ungewoehnlich-niedrige-angebote/
22	Código dos contratos públicos aprovado pelo Decreto-Lei nº 18/2008, de 29 de janeiro, Article 71. URL: https://diariodarepublica.pt/dr/detalhe/decreto-lei/18-2008-248178
23	Public Procurement Law of 2019 as amended - consolidated text 2022, Article 224. URL: https://www.gov.pl/web/uzp-en/legal-framework2
24	Legislative Decree No. 36/2023, Artikel 110. URL: https://www.normattiva.it/uri-res/N2Ls?urn:nir:stato:decreto.legislativo:2023;036
25	Europäische Kommission. Green Public Procurement. URL: https://green-business.ec.europa.eu/green-public-procurement_en
26	Tony Zemaitis Associates Ltd. Understanding Tender Evaluation Criteria. URL: https://www.zemaitis-uk.com/tender-evaluation-criteria/

www.ingramcontent.com/pod-product-compliance
Lightning Source LLC
Chambersburg PA
CBHW071109240526
45469CB00006BD/2400